Original title:
The Dreamland Express

Copyright © 2024 Creative Arts Management OÜ
All rights reserved.

Author: Elliot Harrison
ISBN HARDBACK: 978-9916-90-534-0
ISBN PAPERBACK: 978-9916-90-535-7

Serene Stations in a Dreamscape

At dawn's first light, I softly tread,
In quiet spaces where visions spread.
Each moment lingers, time transcends,
In tranquil places where silence bends.

Shadows dance on walls of gray,
Whispering secrets, they gently sway.
A palette rich in hues so pure,
In this dreamscape, I find my cure.

Veils of mist drift and embrace,
Guiding footsteps at a gentle pace.
Among the echoes, spirits soar,
In serene stations, forevermore.

Awake, yet lost in a hazy trance,
Bound by rhythms of a timeless dance.
The heart beats softly, the soul takes flight,
In this dreamscape, all feels right.

Neon Nights and Whispered Dreams

Neon lights flicker in velvet air,
Casting shadows everywhere.
The city hums a sultry tune,
While stars twinkle beneath the moon.

Whispers float on the evening breeze,
Stories hidden in rustling leaves.
Every corner, a tale unfolds,
In vibrant hues, the night beholds.

Dreams entwine like dappled streams,
Flowing softly through echoed dreams.
Lost in wonder, I take a dive,
In neon nights, I feel alive.

Laughter rings through alley's twist,
Moments captured, moments missed.
With every heartbeat, I roam free,
In whispered dreams, I'm meant to be.

Undulating Thoughts on Iridescent Tracks

Thoughts undulate like waves on sand,
Glimmers of light at the heart's command.
In twilight's glow, perceptions shift,
On tracks of color where shadows drift.

A journey unfolds with every sigh,
As time unravels and dreams comply.
I ride the currents of whispered pleas,
Finding solace in vibrant trees.

In spirals of fate, I'm gently caught,
Chasing echoes of what I sought.
With every twist, I dance and sway,
On iridescent tracks, I find my way.

The night beckons with secrets bright,
Guiding the wanderer with pure delight.
Each moment treasured, each breath a gift,
As undulating thoughts with my heart uplift.

Travelogue of a Nightly Sojourn

In distant lands where shadows lie,
I roam the streets beneath the sky.
Each corner turned, a story waits,
In whispered lore of ancient gates.

The moon, a guide in silver light,
Illuminates paths through the night.
Stars above twinkle like old friends,
Sharing secrets as darkness blends.

Through bustling markets, scents entwine,
Flavorful bites, each one divine.
With laughter shared, and dreams in flight,
A travelogue of a nightly sojourn, bright.

In every heart, a journey sings,
With cherished memories that time brings.
Through winding roads, I'm never alone,
In this adventure, I've found my home.

Fantasies on the Route of Dreams

In shadows deep where secrets dwell,
A whisper blooms, the stories swell.
Through starlit paths of silver beams,
I wander lost in stitched-up dreams.

The moonlight weaves a tender dance,
With every glance, a fleeting chance.
Gossamer thoughts like clouds drift by,
In these realms where hopes can fly.

Mirages sing of distant lands,
With painted skies and gentle sands.
Each echo calls, a siren's plea,
Inviting souls to wander free.

Across the night, where visions gleam,
Reality fades like a silver stream.
In every heartbeat, fantasies gleam,
Awakening life, igniting the dream.

Experience Beyond the Dim Horizon

A horizon glows with heavy sighs,
Where twilight whispers and shadows rise.
Beyond the bounds of earthly sight,
Lies mystery wrapped in deepening night.

Each step I take, the world dissolves,
In colors rich, as the mind evolves.
The stars unveil tales yet untold,
In the calm embrace of stories bold.

With every breath, I break the mold,
Taste the silence, let the truth unfold.
In silence deep, solace I find,
A tapestry spun from heart and mind.

The journey calls, a beckoning hand,
To explore the realms, to understand.
Beyond the confines of what is known,
I stand, embraced by the vast unknown.

Voyage on the Edge of Realities

On the edge where dreams collide,
I sail the waves of the vast divide.
With sails of thought and winds of night,
I traverse realms bathed in soft light.

Waves of wonder, rising high,
In every crest, a glimmering sky.
Through fleeting visions, I carve my way,
In worlds unseen, where shadows play.

Moments flutter like moths to flame,
Each heartbeat whispers a secret name.
Across the void, I dare to roam,
In the tapestry of the unknown home.

The horizon beckons, a siren's call,
To leap into realms where shadows fall.
Here dreams entwine, and fate is spun,
On the edge of realities, the journey's fun.

Midnight Chimeras and Firefly Trails

In the hush of midnight's cloistered dream,
Chimeras roam in a silver gleam.
With fireflies trailing their luminescent flight,
They dance through woods, igniting the night.

Beneath the boughs where echoes play,
Whispers of magic linger and sway.
Each flicker paints a path unseen,
In the depths of darkness, light intervenes.

Figures dart through twisted trees,
Carving journeys on a playful breeze.
With hearts alight and minds astray,
We tread the trails where night holds sway.

In this twilight realm, all fears dissolve,
With chimeras' grace, our dreams evolve.
Under the stars, we find our fate,
In midnight's arms, we celebrate.

Sleepy Cinders and Celestial Views

In the hush of night's embrace,
Stars twinkle in the vast space.
Dreams whisper soft and light,
As fireflies dance in the night.

Echoes of the day now fade,
In moonlit gardens, memories laid.
Cinders ash, a gentle glow,
Cradled by the arms of woe.

Wistful sighs in shadows play,
Guiding souls on their way.
Silhouettes, they beckon near,
In the dark, they shed a tear.

Underneath a cosmos bright,
Sleepy hearts take to flight.
In the slumber, fears disband,
With the night, we're hand in hand.

Twilight Treasures on the Departed Line

At the edge of day's retreat,
Golden hues and shadows meet.
Whispers of the past reside,
In twilight's soft, unending tide.

Glistening secrets, softly shared,
Memories held, though none declared.
Time slips by on silken threads,
As twilight dances, quietly spreads.

Echoes linger, lost and found,
On the departed's gentle ground.
Treasures born of dusk's embrace,
In every shadow, every space.

Hope's last light begins to fade,
While dreams of dusk in silence wade.
In the twilight's tender grace,
The unveiled heart finds its place.

The Night's Vagrant Voyage

Underneath the moon's soft gaze,
Stars embark on secret ways.
Wandering spirits take their flight,
Charting paths in the velvet night.

Whispers carried on the breeze,
Gentle echoes, rustling leaves.
In the dark, they sing their tune,
A vagrant's song beneath the moon.

Every shadow holds a dream,
A fleeting thought, a silver beam.
Together lost, together free,
In night's embrace, we cease to be.

Journeying through skies of ink,
We find the places that we think.
As night unfolds its mystic guise,
In starlit realms, our spirits rise.

Sleep's Shimmering Expressway

Along the road where dreamers drift,
Moonlight weaves a shining gift.
Each star a mile, a journey sweet,
In slumber's glow, hearts find their beat.

Waves of night caress the mind,
In eager silence, treasures find.
The shimmering path calls us near,
To places wrapped in dreams so clear.

Footfalls soft on stardust trails,
Amidst the whispers, love prevails.
Together on this winding way,
In sleep's embrace, we long to stay.

Gliding down this velvet lane,
In dreamscape's soft and sweet refrain.
With every breath, the night we trace,
In shimmering joy, we find our place.

Enchanted Transfers Through the Ether

Whispers travel on the breeze,
Carrying secrets with such ease.
Stars align in cosmic dance,
Unlocking wonders, a fleeting chance.

Dreamers gaze at twilight's glow,
Imagining places only they know.
Threads of light entwine and weave,
In this realm, we'll never leave.

Voices echo, soft and clear,
In the silence, magic's near.
Floating lightly, hearts take flight,
Through the ether, into the night.

Time stands still in this embrace,
As we wander through endless space.
With every heartbeat, a new scene,
In enchanted realms, forever seen.

Sleepless Horizons and Midnight Stops

Midnight whispers through the leaves,
A restless heart, the night deceives.
Horizons stretch with endless dreams,
Each moment bursting at the seams.

Stars like lanterns flicker soft,
Guiding souls that drift aloft.
In shadows deep, reflections play,
While time before us slips away.

Silent streets and echoing sighs,
Awake beneath the velvety skies.
Footfalls dance on cobblestone,
In these hours, we're not alone.

Chasing dawn with eager pace,
Feathers of light, a warm embrace.
In sleepless nights, our spirits soar,
Finding magic, forevermore.

Lullabies Under the Glistening Sky

Underneath the starry dome,
Moonlight bathes the world in gloam.
Whispers soft, a soothing plea,
Lullabies in harmony.

Night unfolds its velvet cloak,
As dreams awaken, gently spoke.
Crickets sing their nightly song,
In nature's arms, where we belong.

Glistening skies, a canvas bright,
Painting wonders in the night.
Hearts entwined, we close our eyes,
Lost together under skies.

Floating on the waves of night,
Embracing peace, a pure delight.
Each sigh, a whisper from above,
Wrapped in dreams and endless love.

Chasing Shadows at Dusk

As daylight fades into a sigh,
Shadows dance and flicker high.
Colors merge in twilight's grace,
Chasing shadows, we find our place.

Whirling leaves, the autumn air,
A fleeting glance, a secret dare.
With every step, we glide and sway,
In the dusk, where dreams hold sway.

Faint echoes of laughter call,
As daylight's curtain begins to fall.
Beneath the trees, we make a wish,
Chasing moments, sweet and swish.

The night awaits with open arms,
In twilight's glow, we find our charms.
Together lost, we'll take our flight,
Chasing shadows into the night.

Aboard the Sleeper of Imagination

In whispers soft, we sail the night,
Through realms where day meets fading light.
Aboard the dreams that weave and spin,
The heart's wild journeys, let them begin.

With shadows cast and visions bright,
We drift through stories, pure delight.
Each thought a star, a spark of grace,
On winding paths, we find our place.

The moonlight sparkles on our skin,
In timeless tales we dive within.
Beyond the borders of the real,
In every dream, our truths reveal.

So close your eyes, embrace the peace,
In realms where vibrant wonders cease.
Aboard the sleeper, souls take flight,
In imagination's wondrous night.

Chasing Dreams Through Celestial Valleys

In twilight's glow, we race the stars,
Through valleys deep, past Jupiter's bars.
With comet tails, we chase the night,
Where dreams take form in endless flight.

Galaxies swirl in colors bright,
We dance on beams of silver light.
With every step, our hearts ignite,
Chasing the echoes of pure delight.

The universe whispers, 'Come and play,'
In cosmic pools where stardust lay.
We gather wishes, dreams anew,
In celestial valleys, skies so blue.

Together we'll weave a tapestry,
Of hopes and visions, wild and free.
Through every moment, hand in hand,
In chasing dreams, we'll make our stand.

Twilight's Expressway

Beneath the skies where shadows dwell,
We travel roads that time can't tell.
On twilight's path, the stars collide,
An expressway where dreams abide.

With whispered words, the night awakes,
As heartbeats quicken, life remakes.
Each turn we take, new wonders found,
In twilight's grasp, our souls unbound.

The horizon blushes, fire aglow,
Through secret alleys, we gently flow.
Adventure calls, we heed its song,
On twilight's expressway, we belong.

In every heartbeat, stories grow,
As time unfolds in a gentle flow.
With open minds, we ride the wave,
On twilight's road, our spirits brave.

Journey of the Stardust Riders

Across the sky, we sail on dreams,
The stardust riders, bold and free.
With laughter bright, we pierce the night,
In cosmic waves of harmony.

We leap from star to shining star,
With tales of hope from near and far.
Together we weave a brilliant dance,
In galaxies kissed by chance.

Nebulas cradle our wildest wishes,
In every burst, a world that glistens.
Through cosmic gardens, we roam wide,
Embracing joy as our faithful guide.

With every journey, hearts unite,
In stardust's glow, we chase the light.
Together we'll brave the endless seas,
For we are stardust, wild and free.

The Night Train to Wonder

In the stillness of the night,
The train whispers through the dark,
Carrying dreams in every light,
As shadows dance like a spark.

Windows glitter like the stars,
Passengers with tales to share,
Each click-clack sings of afar,
Where hearts can breathe and dare.

The engine hums a lullaby,
While mountains bow to moonlit skies,
And as we roll, our spirits fly,
To places where imagination lies.

With every mile, new worlds unfold,
A journey wrapped in night's embrace,
In mysteries of stories told,
We find both peace and endless grace.

Shadows and Secrets on the Rails

Beneath the moon's hush, they glide,
The trains, like dreams, pass side by side,
With shadows slipping through the night,
Each secret waits to take its flight.

A whisper travels on the breeze,
Of lovers lost and fading pleas,
In carriages where hopes reside,
Between the tracks, the dark confides.

The rhythmic beat, a haunting sound,
Echoes through woods, the lost are found,
In journeys long, where souls might weep,
The lines of fate and secrets keep.

As dawn draws near, the tales recede,
Yet every heart rides with a need,
To catch the light, to face the day,
And find the paths where shadows play.

Riding the Tides of Fancy

On ocean waves of bright delight,
A train rides through the dunes of gold,
With every turn, new sparks ignite,
And stories of the sea unfold.

The wind sings soft through open doors,
With laughter dancing in the air,
The rhythm of the surf restores,
Hearts tethered through the journey's care.

Each seat a window to the dreams,
Where fantasies come alive and twirl,
In this world, nothing as it seems,
As imagination spins and swirls.

Through painted skies and breezy lanes,
We travel light, with spirits bold,
In every wave, the heart regains,
A sense of wonder to behold.

Scenic Routes Through Inner Worlds

Through mind's eye, a landscape grows,
A train departs on thought's embrace,
Where every turn, a new path shows,
With vistas painted, full of grace.

The tracks run deep within the soul,
Each click and clack a heart's refrain,
As dreams and fears begin to roll,
Through valleys bright and shadowed plain.

In silence, echoes hum and call,
Reminders of what we can be,
Each stop a chance, where shadows fall,
To glimpse both struggle and the free.

So take this ride, embrace the change,
In every scene, a truth unfurls,
On scenic routes, we find the strange,
In inner realms, our spirit whirls.

Bound for the Realm of Fantasies

In dreams we fly on wings so wide,
Lost in a world where hopes abide.
Colors dance in the soft moonlight,
Every heart sings, a sweet delight.

Magic whispers through the trees,
Promises echo on the breeze.
With each step, new paths unfold,
Stories waiting to be told.

A shimmering lake where fairies glide,
Invisible bridges, a joyful ride.
Stars above like diamonds shine,
Guiding our way through realms divine.

In this land, all troubles cease,
Boundless joy, eternal peace.
Together we'll chase the setting sun,
In fantasies where we are one.

Traverse Through Midnight Whispers

In the quietest hours of night,
Secrets linger, cloaked in light.
Shadows weave a tale so grand,
Holding dreams in a gentle hand.

Echoes softly fill the air,
Of forgotten songs, beyond compare.
The moon above, a watchful eye,
Guides each traveler as they sigh.

Wandering paths of silken dreams,
Lost in thoughts as soft as beams.
Time suspends as wishes breathe,
In the stillness, hearts believe.

With every whisper, tales arise,
Of ancient lore beneath the skies.
In midnight's glow, we find our way,
Bound for tomorrow, come what may.

Beyond the Gates of Imagined Places

In realms where only dreamers tread,
Beyond the gates, our spirits spread.
Vivid hues of distant lands,
Crafting wonders with tender hands.

Mountains rise with timeless grace,
Each stone holds a sacred space.
Rivers hum a lullaby,
Flowing smoothly, never shy.

With every step, new worlds appear,
Whispers calling, drawing near.
A tapestry of thoughts untold,
In this journey, hearts unfold.

Through the gates, we'll wander free,
In imagined places meant to be.
With love and hope, we will embrace,
The magic found in every space.

Odysseys Under the Cosmic Sky

Under the stars, our dreams ignite,
Guided by the celestial light.
Galaxies swirl in dances bold,
Tales of adventure waiting to unfold.

With every comet that streaks by,
We chart our course, inspired to fly.
Nebulas whisper through the night,
Calling out with a shimmering light.

In this vast, uncharted sea,
We sail on hope, wild and free.
Planets hum a timeless song,
In the cosmos, where we belong.

So let us roam, hand in hand,
Through the universe, vast and grand.
Odysseys await, so clear and bright,
Under the cosmic, twinkling light.

Passage to Serendipity

In quiet moments, dreams unfold,
A whisper of fate, soft and bold.
Each path we take, a twist of grace,
Leading us to a wondrous place.

Beneath the stars, we find our way,
Through hidden doors, where wishes play.
Chance embraces, hearts align,
In the tapestry of the divine.

With each new dawn, a chance reborn,
To dance with shadows, the unknown sworn.
Life's gentle nudge, a guiding hand,
Inviting us to understand.

So let us wander, side by side,
Through life's labyrinth, open wide.
For in each moment, joy is found,
In serendipity's sweet surround.

Twilight Adventures Beyond the Stars

At dusk we sail on oceans bright,
Through stratospheres veiled in light.
Galaxies spin, stories told,
In cosmic realms, our dreams unfold.

The Milky Way, our guiding line,
Where starlit secrets intertwine.
With every breath, the universe sings,
A harmony of celestial things.

Comets race on paths of fire,
Fueling hearts with wild desire.
Beyond the veil, where wonders lie,
We chase the dusk, and kiss the sky.

In twilight's embrace, we soar and roam,
Creating legends, far from home.
As night descends, our spirits rise,
Adventurers under endless skies.

Voyages in Sleep's Embrace

In slumber's grip, we drift away,
To lands where dreams forever play.
On gentle waves of midnight's tide,
Where whispers of the heart abide.

Through silver clouds, our spirits glide,
With every breath, our fears subside.
In realms of thought, a vivid dance,
Where shadows twirl in evening's trance.

Mountains rise and rivers flow,
In landscapes crafted soft and slow.
Awakening to secrets deep,
In the sacred silence of our sleep.

With morning's light, our journeys fade,
Yet echoes of the night won't trade.
For in our minds, those voyages gleam,
A tapestry woven from our dream.

Enthralled by Cosmic Tracks

A symphony of stars calls out,
With cosmic trails that dance about.
In the quiet night, we hear the sound,
Of mysteries in the void unbound.

The universe, vast and grand,
Draws us close with a gentle hand.
Each pulse of light, a story shared,
Of countless souls that once dared.

Time unwinds in the cosmic sea,
Where every heart can roam and be.
A voyage through the astral glow,
Where dreams and destinies evolve and flow.

Enthralled by tracks of ancient light,
We journey forth into the night.
For in each star, a spark exists,
To guide us through the cosmic mist.

Essence of Nighttime Rides

The moonlight guides my way,
As shadows softly dance.
With whispers of the night,
I embrace this fleeting chance.

The stars above like gems shine,
In the velvet sky, they gleam.
The world unfolds in whispers,
Awash in a silent dream.

Each turn reveals a secret,
A story lost in time.
The essence of the night,
Carries life in every rhyme.

My heart beats with the engine,
In harmony, we glide.
Through paths of fate and fortune,
In the essence of the ride.

The Journey Beyond the Veil

Beyond the veil of silence,
Where dreams and echoes meet.
A realm of mystic wonders,
Where shadows intertwine fleet.

Guided by an unseen hand,
We drift on currents strange.
With each breath, a new horizon,
In flavors of the change.

The whispers of the ancients,
In every breeze and sigh.
Unraveling the fabric,
Of the night's deep, starlit sky.

Walk with me through stardust,
As time begins to bend.
For in this splendid journey,
The soul will find its end.

The Surreal Expressway

On the surreal expressway,
Where colors blend and swirl.
Reality is distorted,
In this strange, enchanting world.

Winding roads of dreams unfold,
Beneath a sky of thought.
Each sign a vague suggestion,
Of the treasures life has sought.

Mirages dance like phantoms,
In the shimmering heat.
With every mile a vision,
As past and present meet.

Soaring through the twilight,
On this path less defined.
The surreal expressway calls,
Where heart and mind align.

Tracks of the Dreamcatcher

On tracks of the dreamcatcher,
We wander through the night.
Each thread a woven story,
In the soft, magical light.

With every heartbeat captured,
And every wish released.
The dreams entwine like branches,
In the heart of the feast.

Through forests of enchantment,
Where shadows softly play.
The tracks of endless dreaming,
Guide us on our way.

In the stillness, we find comfort,
In the chase of the unknown.
The tracks of the dreamcatcher,
Lead us gently home.

Soaring Through Illusive Realms

In skies where shadows dance and play,
Eagles glide on winds of gray.
Each whisper holds a mystery,
As dreams unfold in history.

Through valleys lost and mountains high,
We chase the whispers of the sky.
With hearts ablaze, we seek the light,
In realms unseen, in endless flight.

The stars align in cosmic grace,
Guiding those who seek their place.
We plunge into the mystic streams,
Soaring ever through our dreams.

With courage found in every breath,
We leave behind all fears of death.
For in the skies, our spirits free,
We journey on eternally.

Whispered Dreams on Silver Rails

Through twilight paths of shimmering light,
Whispers guide our way, so bright.
Silver rails beneath our feet,
Where echoed dreams and visions meet.

With every turn, new tales unfold,
In journeys rich, the heart grows bold.
Together bound by fate's embrace,
We chase the dreams we dare to chase.

The night ignites with stardust gleam,
Awakening our deepest dream.
Whispers weave through trees so tall,
In silver journeys, we hear the call.

As morning breaks, the music plays,
Leading us through wondrous days.
With hearts attuned to every rail,
We ride on through the whispered trail.

Journey into the Clouded Horizon

Beyond horizons, gray and blue,
Lies a journey yet to pursue.
With clouds as maps in the sky above,
We wander forth in search of love.

The whispers of the winds invite,
As day turns softly into night.
With every step, the path grows clear,
In clouded dreams, we shed our fear.

We navigate through mist and fog,
Embracing every. fleeting huddled log.
The horizon beckons, ever near,
Promising peace, and joy sincere.

Through winding trails and shadows cast,
We seek the future, leave the past.
A journey deep into the soul,
Where dreams converge and spirits whole.

The Allure of Endless Journeys

In the heart of each wanderer's quest,
Lies an allure that knows no rest.
Across vast seas and barren lands,
Every moment, destiny stands.

With every dawn, a chance to roam,
Seeking the unknown, far from home.
In every step, a story grows,
As the river of time gently flows.

Elusive paths and winding trails,
Whisper secrets as adventure sails.
With eyes wide open, we embrace,
The journey's thrill and its grace.

For in each heartbeat lies the prize,
A chance to dream beneath the skies.
The allure of endless journeys calls,
To every spirit, it enthralls.

The Journey of Endless Dreams

In twilight's calm embrace, we drift,
Chasing shadows of our past,
With every step, our spirits lift,
Towards horizons vast and fast.

A compass made of whispered hopes,
Guides our hearts through unseen streams,
We find our way with tangled ropes,
Entwined within our endless dreams.

The stars align, their paths we trace,
As constellations weave our fate,
Each glance unveils a secret place,
Where destiny and chance await.

With every dawn, new visions bloom,
A canvas painted in the light,
We wander far beyond the gloom,
Embarking on this wondrous flight.

Celestial Serendipity

Beneath the vast and velvet skies,
Lies a spark that flickers bright,
In serendipity, truth lies,
Guiding dreams to purest light.

The dance of planets, sweet and slow,
Whispers secrets in the night,
With every twinkle, they bestow,
A chance encounter, pure delight.

Galaxies spin in cosmic tune,
As stardust flutters in our wake,
We sail on winds that sing the moon,
In search of joy, for love's own sake.

Each moment shared, a precious gift,
Carried on the wings of fate,
Through every turn, our spirits lift,
In this universe, we create.

Ascending The Night's Currents

With twilight's breeze upon our skin,
We rise on currents of the night,
In whispered dreams, our journey begins,
    Carried forth by starry light.

The moonlight casts a silver glow,
As shadows dance in mystic air,
We follow where the wild winds blow,
    Untamed spirits, free from care.

Across the sky we weave and spin,
With hopes entwined in every breath,
In each embrace, new tales begin,
Through life, through love, until our death.

As daylight fades, we won't retreat,
Embracing all the night can bring,
Ascend with joy, our hearts repeat,
    The melody of stars that sing.

The Cartography of Dreams

In the atlas of our minds, we chart,
Paths untraveled, rivers wide,
Every line, a work of art,
As we navigate the tide.

With ink of hope, we sketch our fate,
Mountains rise, and valleys fall,
In every corner, we await,
The magic of our dreamer's call.

Navigating through fears and schemes,
We find the treasures hid inside,
Each twist reveals our deepest dreams,
A journey that we must confide.

The world unfolds beneath our feet,
Together, hand in hand we stand,
In this cartography, we meet,
A tale of love, a life unplanned.

Boundless Valleys of the Mind's Eye

In valleys deep where thoughts do dwell,
The whispers dance, they weave, they tell.
Of dreams once lost, of hopes reborn,
In every shadow, a light is worn.

The river flows with silent grace,
Through winding paths, it finds its place.
Each turn reveals a story's thread,
Where echoes linger, softly spread.

Mountains rise in silent might,
Guarding secrets of day and night.
With every step, the heart takes flight,
In boundless realms of pure delight.

Embrace the journey, let it flow,
Through valleys deep, where dreams will grow.
With every thought, a world unspun,
In mind's vast eye, we are all one.

Destinations of Starlit Reverie

Beneath the stars, our dreams take flight,
A tapestry of endless night.
Each twinkle speaks a cosmic call,
In whispered tones, we feel it all.

The moonlit path is ours to roam,
In celestial realms, we'll find a home.
With every step, our spirits rise,
To dance among the tranquil skies.

Galaxies swirl in a cosmic embrace,
In this vastness, we find our place.
With every heartbeat, we ignite,
Destinations filled with purest light.

Let reverie guide our wayward quest,
In starlit dreams, we find our rest.
As we traverse this endless sea,
Our hearts will soar, forever free.

Ephemeral Escapades Through the Void

In shadows cast by fleeting time,
We chase the echoes, soft and prime.
Each moment slips like grains of sand,
In the void's embrace, we take a stand.

Through whispered winds, our spirits sail,
On currents bright, we cannot fail.
With every breath, a world begins,
In ephemeral dance, our journey spins.

Stars will guide our wandering hearts,
In the silence, each tale imparts.
As visions blend in twilight's grace,
We find ourselves in time's soft chase.

Embrace the fleeting, cherish the now,
In each transient moment, we take a bow.
Through the void, we'll glide and play,
In escapades that fade away.

Routes of Reverie Under Glittering Canopies

Under canopies of shimmering light,
We wander paths of pure delight.
Each leaf a portal, each branch a dream,
In nature's arms, our souls will gleam.

The air is filled with laughter's song,
In this realm, we all belong.
With every step, the earth will sigh,
As whispered wonders drift on by.

Boundless routes of thought explore,
With every turn, there's so much more.
In reverie's glow, we'll find our way,
Through glittering nights and golden day.

So take my hand, let's wander free,
In this tapestry of destiny.
Through dreams we chase and hearts that soar,
Under the stars, forevermore.

Whispers of the Midnight Train

In shadows deep, the train rolls slow,
A lullaby sings where soft winds blow.
Stars above twinkle, a guiding light,
Whispers of dreams in the quiet night.

Carriages sway with tales untold,
Each traveler lost, their secrets unfold.
Through valleys wide and mountains steep,
Mysteries awaken, from slumber deep.

The clatter of wheels, a soothing sound,
In this silver cocoon, enchantment is found.
Moments drift by like drifting smoke,
As memories dance, and shadows evoke.

Silent companions on this journey shared,
Hearts intertwine, as thoughts are bared.
The midnight train knows the paths we tread,
With every whisper, our spirits are fed.

Journeys Through Somnolent Realms

In dreams we ride on starlit beams,
Through realms of slumber, we weave our themes.
Fields of twilight, glowing with grace,
Adventures await in this timeless place.

Lost in big cities, shadows collide,
Each turn reveals what the heart can't hide.
Voices echo in the still of night,
Guiding us softly towards the light.

With gentle rhythms, the stories blend,
In this endless journey, there's no end.
Emotions linger on the softest breeze,
As we meander with effortless ease.

Awake or asleep, we find our way,
Through somnolent realms where wishes sway.
In dreams we travel, in dreams we stay,
Chasing the night till the break of day.

Tracks of Whimsy and Wonder

Upon the tracks, where dreams ignite,
The whimsy of youth takes to flight.
A carousel of laughter and play,
Under the stars, we dance and sway.

Each station holds a secret to share,
With a gust of wind, we breathe the air.
Between the carriages, we shall roam,
Finding magic in the unknown home.

Through forests thick and rivers wide,
On tracks of wonder, we shall glide.
Every rustle holds a tale profound,
In the heart of night, enchantment is found.

Moments collide, like flashes of light,
In the fleeting hours before dawn's flight.
On tracks of whimsy, forever we'll stay,
Chasing the dreams that beckon our way.

Midnight Adventures on Silver Rails

At the stroke of twelve, the journey begins,
Under the moon, where silence wins.
Silver rails shimmer, a beckoning hue,
Drawing us forth to explore the new.

Through sleepy towns, where shadows lay,
Across the landscape, we dance and sway.
Hearts filled with joy, our spirits free,
On midnight adventures, just you and me.

Every whistle carries a tale so sweet,
Of lovers and dreamers that fate will meet.
In the cool night air, we laugh and sing,
Finding the magic that each moment brings.

Through teeming stars and endless skies,
We chase the horizon where freedom lies.
With every mile, a new dream revealed,
On silver rails, our fate is sealed.

The Night Train's Lullaby

The whistle sings a gentle tune,
As shadows play beneath the moon.
The wheels keep rolling, soft and slow,
While dreams begin to softly flow.

The lights slip by in fleeting gleam,
A world that beckons us to dream.
Each passenger, a story lost,
On this warm train, we count the cost.

The night, it wraps us in its arms,
While silence charms and softly calms.
Outside the window, stars glide by,
Together we shall soar and fly.

So close your eyes, let visions play,
As we drift far from the day.
The train keeps rolling, heartbeats sway,
In night's embrace, we find our way.

Odyssey Through the Land of Nod

In twilight's grasp, we take our flight,
To realms where dreams ignite the night.
Each step a tale, both wild and free,
In land where wishes want to be.

The whispers call, a siren's sound,
Through valleys deep and hills unbound.
We wander lost in shadows' glow,
With every moment, time must slow.

The moonlight bathes the landscape fair,
With magic woven through the air.
A dance of spirits in the mist,
In every twirl, a dream is kissed.

As dawn approaches, colors blend,
Our journey nears its bitter end.
But in our hearts, this night will stay,
A treasure wrought from dreams' ballet.

Celestial Junctions in the Dream World

Stars align in patterns bright,
Guiding souls through the endless night.
Galaxies whirl in graceful spins,
In dreams, the universe begins.

Nebulas bloom with colors vast,
Each moment echoes from the past.
Portals open, paths unfold,
In dream's embrace, a tale retold.

We drift through realms of cosmic light,
Where fantasies take shape and flight.
Visions spark in wondrous sights,
The heart unchains, and hope ignites.

As morning claims the starry sky,
With a soft yawn, we say goodbye.
Yet in our minds, those dreams remain,
A tapestry of quiet refrains.

Whispers of Moonlit Journeys

Beneath the moon's enchanting glow,
We wander paths where soft winds blow.
With every step, the night will sing,
Of secret dreams that twilight brings.

The forest hums a soothing tune,
While shadows dance beneath the moon.
Each rustling leaf, a soft embrace,
In dreams, we find our sacred place.

Stars twinkle high, their stories old,
With every glance, their tales unfold.
We follow trails of silver light,
As whispers guide us through the night.

So close your eyes and take my hand,
Together we will understand.
This moonlit journey, ours to share,
In dreams' embrace, we lose our care.

Railways of the Ethereal Kingdom

In the land where shadows glide,
Steel and dreams intertwine.
Whispers of the stars collide,
Journeys penned in silver line.

Carriages of light they ride,
Through the mist of ancient lore.
Each station calls with vibrant pride,
To secrets locked behind each door.

Wanderers with hearts set free,
On tracks that spark the night anew.
They chase the dawn's soft melody,
In a kingdom painted in deep blue.

Through valleys of celestial gold,
Rumbles softly, a train of thought.
Adventures waiting to unfold,
In the realms where dreams are sought.

The Realm of Sleepy Wanderings

In the dusk where shadows creep,
Lies a world that slumbers deep.
Wanderers drift on whispered sighs,
In the realm 'neath twilight skies.

Clouds like pillows gently nest,
Softly cradling every quest.
Footsteps echo, muted, slow,
In the lands where soft dreams flow.

Moonlit paths with silver beams,
Guide the hearts of slumbering dreams.
Each corner turned, a new delight,
In the hush that wraps the night.

Stars above, a watchful throng,
Sing the wanderers' soft song.
In this realm of sleepy grace,
They find solace, time and space.

Embarking on Nocturnal Explorations

Beneath the veil of night so still,
Adventurers chase the silent thrill.
Through shadows where the secrets lie,
They walk beneath the vast, dark sky.

Each step a whisper on the ground,
In this world, where dreams are found.
Stars are guides, in silver hues,
As they wander through cosmic views.

When the moon spills its gentle light,
Curiosity sparks in the night.
To distant lands their spirits soar,
Embarking on paths unseen before.

With every heartbeat, the night unfolds,
A tapestry of stories told.
They journey forth, hand in hand,
In the realm of night's endless land.

Surreal Journeys through the Night's Canvas

In shadows deep, the silence hums,
Whispers sketching dreams that come.
Colors swirl in twilight's glow,
Each brushstroke holds a tale to show.

Waves of stars in velvet skies,
Dancing lights, where magic lies.
Paths of wonder, sights unseen,
Unraveled threads of what has been.

Eyes wide open, hearts set free,
Floating on a cosmic sea.
Time bends softly, night unfolds,
In this realm, no one gets old.

Beneath the moon's enchanting gaze,
We wander through this endless maze.
A canvas rich with midnight dreams,
In surreal journeys, nothing seems.

A Playground of Starry Visions

Beneath the arch of night's embrace,
We leap into a time and space.
Galaxies spin, a vibrant tide,
In shadows where our dreams reside.

Nebulas bloom like flowers bright,
Sparks of joy in pure delight.
We chase the comets, glide and play,
In playgrounds where the stardust lay.

Each twinkle holds a story spun,
Echoes of laughter, all in fun.
Boundless worlds await our quest,
In the heart of night, we find our rest.

Through cosmic slides and moonlit swings,
We dance on air and spread our wings.
A playground vast, our spirits soar,
In starry visions, forevermore.

Tracks Through the Dream Weaver's Hall

In halls of dreams, where echoes dwell,
Time weaves tales, a mystic spell.
Footprints mark the path we take,
Through veils of night that softly shake.

Threads of silver, whispers soft,
Guide us gently, lift us aloft.
Past doors adorned with twilight's hue,
Each reveal of hope, a vision new.

Mirrors shimmer with faces bright,
Reflecting moments, pure delight.
We wander through this endless maze,
In the dream weaver's tender gaze.

With every step, a story spins,
In reveries where love begins.
Tracks of magic, rich and grand,
In the dreamer's hall, hand in hand.

Nighttime Adventures in Lost Landscapes

In landscapes lost in twilight's glow,
We roam where silent shadows flow.
Mountains rise like ancient kings,
Whispering secrets that night brings.

Rivers glisten in starry beams,
Reflecting all our wildest dreams.
Through hidden paths, we find our way,
In nighttime adventures, come what may.

Fog wraps softly 'round the trees,
Carried by a gentle breeze.
Footsteps echo on the ground,
In these lost lands, magic is found.

We chase the night, embrace the fear,
With every breath, the moment's clear.
In lost landscapes, hearts entwined,
Nighttime adventures, unconfined.

The Timeless Voyage

In the realm where moments blend,
Waves of time, they twist and bend.
Stars above like lanterns glow,
Guiding souls where dreams may flow.

Through the mist, the whispers call,
Echoes soft, they rise and fall.
A ship of thoughts on endless seas,
Sailing forth upon the breeze.

In this dance of dusk and dawn,
Lifetimes pass, yet none are gone.
Every heartbeat, every sigh,
Moments cherished, never die.

As shadows shift and candles wane,
Time's embrace is sweet, not vain.
Onward bound, the voyage goes,
In timeless tales, the spirit flows.

Encounters in the Land of Slumber

In a place where dreams reside,
Silence hums, no fear to bide.
Wandering spirits softly tread,
In the land where night is spread.

Figures dance beneath moonlight,
Glimmers spark in gentle flight.
Whispers speak of tales untold,
Wrapped in rhythms, brave and bold.

Every corner holds a sight,
Creatures born of pure delight.
Join in laughter, gleam with cheer,
In this realm, all dreams are near.

As the dawn begins to creep,
Soft goodbyes, the secrets keep.
Though we part, the dream remains,
In the land where slumber reigns.

Celestial Tracks to Enchantment

Underneath a stardust sky,
Galaxies spin and soar high.
Tracks of light, they weave and sway,
Guiding hearts along the way.

Train of dreams on silver rails,
Carrying hopes that never pale.
Through the cosmos, swift we glide,
On the journey, worlds reside.

Each station holds a brand new scene,
Mystic lands, forever green.
With a pause, the magic starts,
Open roads for wandering hearts.

Endless night, yet paths are bright,
Celestial wonders, pure delight.
With every turn, enchantments call,
Everlasting, we shall fall.

The Fantastical Journey of the Sleep Train

A train of dreams, it rolls tonight,
Chasing stars, embracing light.
Wheels of wishes, softly hum,
Into realms where night is fun.

Carriages filled with whispered tales,
Magical realms where laughter sails.
Celestial maps in every hand,
Together we explore this land.

Through landscapes vast, with colors bold,
Stories of the heart unfold.
Passengers of every kind,
United in the maps we find.

As the dawn begins to greet,
Sleep train rolls on, bittersweet.
Yet in dreams, we'll ride again,
On fantastical paths, amen.

Starlit Paths of the Imagination

Beneath the glow of silver light,
Thoughts take flight, dreams burn bright.
Whispers of worlds yet to be,
Guiding us through reverie.

Winding paths of endless grace,
Each step a new, enchanted place.
Stars align to show the way,
In this night, we wish and sway.

With every twinkle in the skies,
A tapestry of hopes arise.
Imagination's gentle hand,
Crafts a soft and vibrant land.

So let us wander, hearts alive,
In starlit dreams, we will thrive.
Together on this endless ride,
Where fantasies and truth collide.

Echoes in the Night Train

The whistle blows, the journey starts,
Rumbling softly through our hearts.
Carriages filled with whispered tales,
As shadows dance on moonlit trails.

Flickering lights, they guide our gaze,
Through fleeting moments, endless days.
Echoes call from far away,
Memories linger, softly sway.

Wheels keep rolling, time stands still,
A pulse of magic, bend our will.
Each stop a dream, a chance to feel,
The night train's secrets slowly reveal.

So hold on tight, let spirits soar,
In this rhythm, we will explore.
Echoing laughter fills the air,
On this night train, we cast our care.

Fantasies on the Fast Track

Whirling dreams on racing tracks,
Chasing stardust, never slack.
Adventures bloom with every mile,
In this whirlwind, we find our style.

Engines roar, igniting fire,
Our spirits lift, rising higher.
Speeding through the realms of thought,
In this pulse, we find what's sought.

Landscapes blur, yet visions clear,
Fantasies call, drawing near.
With every curve, new worlds to see,
Unraveled dreams set our minds free.

Thus we ride on tracks of grace,
In our hearts, we find our place.
Fantasies guide the swiftest way,
Together in this bright ballet.

Routes to the Realm of Dreams

Paths unfold beneath the moon,
In twilight's hush, we find our tune.
Each route a thread of silver light,
Leading us to realms of night.

Voices whisper secrets shared,
In this space, our dreams declared.
Mountains high, valleys low,
In the dreamscape, we freely go.

Routes entwined with hopes untold,
Shimmering sights of bright and bold.
Every turn a chance to see,
The wonders of our mystery.

So take my hand, and dare to roam,
In this realm, we find our home.
With every step on golden beams,
We'll wander deep in woven dreams.

Transcendence on the Dreamway

Whispers drift on moonlit streams,
Where thoughts dance like scattered dreams.
Clouds embrace the starry night,
And all is bathed in gentle light.

Footsteps wander on paths of grace,
The heart finds peace in this holy place.
Time's embrace feels soft and wide,
Lost in the flow of the cosmic tide.

Every breath a stitch of fate,
As worlds align and time dilates.
In this realm where spirits soar,
Awakening opens the ancient door.

We soar beyond the limits known,
Transcending worlds we call our own.
In dreams, we gather, hearts aflame,
Forever changed, we speak the same.

Night's Lullaby of Adventure

In the hush of velvet skies,
Whispers call where shadows rise.
Stars ignite with secret tales,
A melody in moonlight sails.

Winds of wonder weave through trees,
Carrying songs upon the breeze.
Every rustle, every sigh,
Holds the promise of the sky.

Journeys whispered soft and sweet,
In reverie, our hearts will meet.
Across the fields of dreams we roam,
The night becomes our sacred home.

With every shadowed step we take,
The world around begins to wake.
Adventures spark beneath our feet,
In night's embrace, our spirits greet.

Mystical Routes of Reverie

Through the mist of twilight's glow,
Ambassadors of dreams do flow.
Paths unseen, yet deeply known,
In quiet grace, our souls have grown.

Fields of awe beneath our gaze,
Boundless realms in magic haze.
Every turn, a wondrous sight,
Journey woven in pure light.

Whispers echo through the trees,
Lost in thoughts that drift like leaves.
In this dance of past and dream,
Life unfolds like a flowing stream.

As we traverse this sacred land,
Hand in hand, we understand.
In intertwining dreams we find,
The map to hearts that love unbind.

The Celestial Locomotive

A train of stars on silver tracks,
Rolling through the darkened cracks.
With every whistle, stories rise,
Crafting worlds beneath the skies.

Passengers of thought and time,
Riding rhythms, pure as rhyme.
Each station a new mystery,
Life's adventure calls to me.

Carriages of dreams unite,
In this realm of endless night.
Glimmers spark as heartbeats thrill,
Onward we go, beyond the hill.

Through the cosmos, we ascend,
A journey with no defined end.
As stars align and hearts ignite,
The celestial train takes flight.

Ghosts of Forgotten Journeys

Whispers cling to the ancient trees,
Echoes of paths worn down by time.
Shadows dance where the memories freeze,
In the air, a melancholic rhyme.

Footsteps fade on the rusted track,
Carried away on a whisper's breath.
Stories linger, never to lack,
Sunk deep in the silence of death.

Lost are the faces that once remained,
Faded like ink upon fragile pages.
Dreams of the travelers, joy uncontained,
Adapt through the years, altering stages.

Yet in the night, their spirits revive,
Guiding the way where the lost now roam.
In the dark, the echoes contrive,
To lead every wanderer back home.

Rails of the Unseen

Winding paths of steel and stone,
Beneath the layers of dusk's embrace.
Journeys taken, yet never shown,
As ghostly trains slide through time and space.

Tracks that shimmer in twilight's grip,
Hearts racing with each gentle sway.
Whistle calls from a phantom ship,
As shadows dance, they find their way.

Secrets held in the iron veins,
Restless dreams travel through the night.
Timeless tales bind the silent chains,
Connecting the lost to the light.

The rails may fade but stories thrive,
In every derailment, hope resides.
Through unseen worlds, we come alive,
Riding the currents where mystery hides.

The Twilight Transcendence

When day dips low, the horizon glows,
A transient world painted in hues.
In twilight's touch, a stillness flows,
As whispers weave through the evening's muse.

The moon emerges with gentle grace,
Softing the edges of lingering fears.
Stars awaken, taking their place,
Guiding the lost through a cascade of tears.

In the silence, time bends just right,
Crimson shadows dance on the wall.
Voices call from the depths of night,
In this stillness, we answer the call.

To transcend in dreams, we must learn,
To let go, give fate a chance.
As twilight fades, we all discern,
The beauty found in our own dance.

Navigating the Starlit Wilderness

Under a dome of cosmic light,
We wander through whispers of the night.
Each flicker guides through the unknown,
As hearts embrace the sounds of the starlit tone.

The paths are thick with mystery's lure,
In the silence, secrets start to stir.
Gentle winds carry tales of old,
In this wilderness, numerous stories unfold.

With every step, wild dreams arise,
A symphony sung by unseen skies.
We navigate through the cosmic sea,
Finding solace in where we are meant to be.

So gather your courage, let spirits ignite,
The starlit wilderness is ours tonight.
In the vastness, we answer the call,
Together we soar, together we fall.

Boundless Journeys Beyond Sleep

In dreams we wander wide and far,
Through forests deep and skies that spar.
With whispers soft that guide our way,
We dance with shadows till break of day.

Each turn unveils a secret place,
Where time stands still, a gentle grace.
With every step, the world anew,
A canvas painted in every hue.

The stars above our hearts ignite,
As we embrace the endless night.
In slumber's arms, we come alive,
With every dream, our spirits thrive.

So close your eyes, let worries fade,
In realms where fantasies are made.
A journey vast, in silence seeped,
We find the wonders boundless, deep.

Cars of Curiosity and Wonder

A whistle blows, the engine roars,
Through twisting tracks and open doors.
Each journey starts with questions bare,
Unraveling tales from everywhere.

With windows wide, we gaze outside,
Where mountains stand and rivers glide.
The stories whispered in the breeze,
Invite us to discover, to seize.

The wheels turn fast, the world unfolds,
In vibrant hues, new dreams retold.
In metal hearts, our hopes reside,
As curiosity becomes our guide.

So let us ride through thought and time,
In cars that chase the hills we climb.
Where wonder grips and hearts take flight,
Each mile a spark, each turn delight.

Stars Beneath the Velvet Ceiling

Beneath the night, a tapestry,
Of dreams that twinkle, wild and free.
The velvet sky, a shroud of grace,
Holds wishes whispered in endless space.

Each star a story, bright and bold,
Of love and loss, of dreams retold.
They flicker soft, like hearts they sing,
A cosmic dance, a sacred ring.

In twilight's grasp, we find our way,
To realms where magic's here to stay.
The universe, our canvas wide,
Where every heart can safely bide.

So close your eyes and catch a dream,
Among the stars, hear their soft gleam.
Beneath the velvet, hope ignites,
In cosmic whispers, endless nights.

The Fantastical Railway of Night

On tracks of silver, shadows glide,
A train of wonder, hearts open wide.
Through valleys deep and mountains high,
We chase the moon across the sky.

With every jolt, a tale unfolds,
Of mystic lands and secrets told.
The whistle calls, our spirits soar,
Through realms of dreams forevermore.

The lanterns glow with stories bright,
They light the path, dispelling fright.
In every car, new friends we find,
In laughter shared, our souls entwined.

So take a seat, let worries flee,
In this fantastical journey, be free.
The railway winds through starry nights,
Where every heart finds pure delights.

Uncharted Paths of the Mind

Through whispers of thought, we wander free,
In twisted corridors, secrets we see.
Each shadow that flickers, a story untold,
In the maze of our minds, adventures unfold.

With every step forward, we dare to explore,
The landscapes of memory, forevermore.
Imagination dances, a flickering flame,
On uncharted paths, we play a new game.

With colors that shimmer and words that ignite,
We traverse the realms of both day and night.
A tapestry woven with dreams held so dear,
In the heart of our minds, we cast off all fear.

So venture within, let your spirit take flight,
Uncharted paths wait in the folds of the night.
The journey is endless, the treasure is bold,
In the chambers of thought, life's wonders unfold.

The Traveler's World of Dreams

In whispers of night, the traveler sighs,
Beneath silver moons and star-speckled skies.
He wanders through visions, both vivid and bright,
In worlds crafted softly by slumber's sweet light.

Through forests of wonder, and fields made of gold,
Each dream is a story waiting to be told.
With footsteps of silk, he dances with fate,
In the traveler's world, there's no room for hate.

Mountains of hope rise against clouds of despair,
In the realm of his dreams, he finds peace in the air.
Every heartbeat echoes, each moment's a breeze,
In this land of the heart, he feels time's gentle tease.

Awake from the night, he carries it near,
The essence of dreams fills his soul with cheer.
A traveler of visions, forever he roams,
In the world of his dreams, he finds his true home.

Navigating the Night's Unknown

Under starlit whispers, the seeker treads slow,
Through shadows that twist where wild winds blow.
With lanterns of hope, they guide his brave heart,
In the night's vast unknown, he plays his small part.

The moon casts a map on the waters so wide,
As secrets awaken, no longer they hide.
With courage in hand, and dreams in his chest,
He sails into darkness, into the great quest.

Each gust of the wind carries stories of old,
Of adventures uncharted, and treasures of gold.
Navigating the unknown with eyes open wide,
In the depths of the night, where mysteries bide.

So come take the plunge, let your spirit ignite,
In the dance of the shadows, embrace the pure light.
For in navigating night's unknown with belief,
We find the true magic hidden in grief.

Train to Imaginary Realms

All aboard the train to where fantasies dwell,
Through tunnels of dreams, on a shimmering swell.
With each clack and clatter, the magic takes flight,
In imaginary realms, we embrace the night.

As landscapes shift softly, like pages in books,
We visit the places that spark joyful looks.
Endless adventures await on the track,
With imagination guiding us, there's no looking back.

From islands of laughter to mountains of tears,
The train takes us forward through hopes and fears.
Each station a treasure, each stop a new chance,
In this whimsical journey, let our hearts dance.

So come join the ride to where wonders shine bright,
On the train to imaginary realms of delight.
Together we'll journey through moments surreal,
In the magic of dreams, our hearts will reveal.

Echoes on the Midnight Train

Whispers travel through the night,
As shadows dance in soft moonlight.
A train rolls on, a fleeting dream,
Where time and space are not as they seem.

Voices linger, stories blend,
In every curve, a journey's end.
Wheels on tracks, a rhythmic song,
Echoes call where hearts belong.

Ghostly figures, faces pale,
Each one tells a secret tale.
Stars above, like watchful eyes,
Guide the way as midnight flies.

Through dim-lit cars, the night unfolds,
In silent prayers, a truth unfolds.
With every stop, a life reborn,
On this train, new dreams are worn.

Tracks of Fantasia

Upon the tracks, the visions weave,
A tapestry of dreams we believe.
Colors swirl in vibrant light,
In this world, our hearts take flight.

Whistles blow through tranquil air,
Magic lingers everywhere.
With every turn, new wonders rise,
In Fantasia, beneath the skies.

Laughter echoes, joy abounds,
Adventure waits in hidden sounds.
Guide us through this endless maze,
Lost in childhood's wistful gaze.

As the engine speeds away,
We'll chase the dawn, come what may.
Through painted landscapes, bold and bright,
On tracks of dreams, we chase the light.

Starlit Odyssey

Beneath the stars, we roam so free,
An endless journey, just you and me.
Galaxies twinkle in the night,
Guiding our hearts with gentle light.

Each step we take, a path unknown,
In starlit dreams, our fate is sown.
Celestial whispers call our name,
In this odyssey, nothing's the same.

Lost in a cosmic, boundless sea,
We dance with fate, wild and carefree.
Wonders unfold with every sight,
In the darkness, we find our light.

Through nebulae, we drift and glide,
Together forever, side by side.
Embracing night, our spirits soar,
In this starlit quest, forevermore.

Boundless Horizons

A canvas stretched beyond the eye,
Where dreams take flight and hopes will fly.
Beyond the edge, the sky unrolls,
In every heart, a story unfolds.

Waves of color, brush the land,
Nature whispers, soft and grand.
Mountains rise, like giants bold,
In their shadows, our dreams are told.

With every sunrise, a brand new chance,
To chase the shadows, to join the dance.
In endless fields, our spirits roam,
Among the stars, we make our home.

Boundless horizons, the world awaits,
With open arms, it serenates.
We'll journey forth, side by side,
Together in life's eternal ride.

Chasing Echoes Through Ethereal Pathways

In shadows where the whispers play,
The echoes dance, they fade away.
Through misty paths of silver light,
We chase them down into the night.

Lost in dreams where memories hide,
Each step reveals the past inside.
With every turn, my heart does race,
Seeking echoes in this space.

The air is thick with tales untold,
In every breath, a wish unfolds.
Through corridors of time we weave,
In chasing echoes, we believe.

A fleeting touch, a soft refrain,
In every echo, joy and pain.
Through ethereal pathways we roam,
In search of what feels like home.

The Luminous Route of Imagination

Through colors bright, where dreams ignite,
Imagination takes its flight.
Each thought a star, each whisper new,
On paths of light, we journey through.

Where reality bends and sways,
In bright hues of fantastical days.
A canvas vast, a world so wide,
In luminous routes, our hopes reside.

With every step, a story grows,
In vibrant tones, our spirit flows.
A tapestry of endless scenes,
In the heart's realm, where brilliance beams.

So let us wander, hand in hand,
Through worlds where only dreams can stand.
On luminous paths, our souls will find,
The treasures held in a vivid mind.

Riding Waves of Silence

In the stillness of the night,
Silence rides a wave of light.
The ocean breathes, so calm and deep,
In its embrace, we drift and sleep.

Whispers rise like gentle foam,
Carrying thoughts of a distant home.
Each wave a pause, a moment brief,
In silence found, we seek relief.

The moonlight shimmers, soft and pale,
Guiding us as we set sail.
With every hush, a secret shared,
In waves of silence, hearts are bared.

Together wrapped in tranquil sound,
In silent depths, our dreams are found.
We ride the currents, free and clear,
Embracing calm, we lose our fear.

Gateway to Dreaming Skies

Beneath the stars, where wishes gleam,
A gateway opens to a dream.
With every glance, the sky unfolds,
A universe of tales untold.

Through velvet night, our spirits soar,
On whispered winds, we seek the shore.
In dreaming skies, we find our place,
With every heartbeat, a gentle grace.

The clouds are driven by our hopes,
In boundless realms, our vision scopes.
A canvas vast, where dreams ignite,
In gateway realms, we chase the light.

So leap with faith into the bright,
And dance among the stars tonight.
For in this space, our dreams align,
And in dreaming skies, our hearts entwine.

Harmonies of the Dreamer's Path

In twilight's glow, the whispers call,
Where shadows dance and echoes stall,
Dreamers tread on paths unseen,
To weave the tales where hopes have been.

With starlit skies to guide their way,
They chase the dawn of a new day,
With every step, the heart will sing,
Along the road where visions spring.

The breeze carries a soothing tune,
As night succumbs to the silver moon,
Each note a promise, soft and clear,
A symphony for those who dare.

In harmony, their spirits soar,
Awakening what's held in store,
For in the dreamer's heart, they find,
A world where every thought's aligned.

Aboard the Vessel of Dreams

A ship of stars on ocean's sway,
With sails of hope, it glides away,
Each wind that blows, a guiding force,
Through realms of joy, it charts its course.

The sky ablaze with colors bright,
As dreams take flight, igniting night,
With every wave, a story told,
Of daring dreams and hearts so bold.

The captain's heart beats strong and true,
With visions vast, and skies so blue,
Together bound, they journey far,
Embraced by every twinkling star.

For once aboard this vessel grand,
The dreamer's wish is in command,
To sail where thoughts and visions gleam,
Forever lost aboard the dream.

Windows to Imaginary Places

Through glassy panes, the stories gleam,
A glimpse into a waking dream,
Each window holds a vision clear,
Of worlds unknown, both far and near.

In forests lush where colors blend,
Or cities bright where journeys end,
They beckon forth with open arms,
To share their wonders, spark their charms.

The whispers of the past unfold,
Historic paths in tales retold,
With every sight, a memory flows,
Of all the paths the heart well knows.

Imaginary realms await,
For those who dare to navigate,
Through windows bright, the dreamers see,
A treasure trove of mystery.

Reflections on the Glimmering Rails

On glimmering rails where shadows play,
Reflections dance in bright array,
Trains of thought glide through the night,
As journeys beckon into light.

Each station marked by hopes once lost,
The price of dreams, a heavy cost,
Yet in the silver beams so bright,
A spark ignites the dark of night.

With whispers low, the engines hum,
A heartbeat strong, a steady drum,
Through valleys deep and mountains high,
The dreamers chase the endless sky.

Reflections swirl in twilight's quest,
A voyage bound, a soul's request,
For on these rails, their hearts entwine,
In every step, their dreams align.

Essence of the Starlit Adventure

Beneath the sky, a canvas wide,
We wander paths where stardust hides.
Each twinkling light, a whispered tale,
Guides our hearts as we set sail.

Through nebulae and cosmic streams,
We chase the echoes of our dreams.
Together we dance, a celestial waltz,
Where time dissolves and silence halts.

The moon a lantern, soft and bright,
Illuminating the velvet night.
In every breath, the universe sings,
With every step, new magic springs.

As dawn awakens, colors blend,
The starlit journey finds its end.
Yet in our hearts, the essence stays,
A memory of those starlit days.

Encapsulated in a Dream

A world where dreams do softly bloom,
In twilight's grasp, we escape the gloom.
Each whispered wish, a feathered flight,
We drift on clouds through the velvet night.

Crystal visions in the moon's pale glow,
Secrets linger where the wild winds blow.
In the silence, echoes of our fears,
Mingle gently with our fleeting years.

Chasing shadows, we find our way,
Through fields of stardust, we wish to stay.
The fabric of night, a comforting seam,
Weaves a tapestry, encapsulated in a dream.

As dawn approaches, colors collide,
Yet in our hearts, the dreams abide.
In every heartbeat, a promise gleams,
A magic that lives in the realm of dreams.

The Enchanted Sleeper

In whispers deep, through twilight's veil,
The enchanted sleeper tells a tale.
With closed eyes, they travel far,
Guided by the light of a wandering star.

Around them dance the night's sweet sighs,
While ancient secrets in slumber rise.
The moonlight weaves through tendrils of night,
Cradling dreams in soft silver light.

Time stands still in this sacred space,
Every heartbeat a lingering trace.
As shadows blend with realms unseen,
Reality fades, and the soul leans in.

Awake or asleep, which path will they choose?
In the dance of night, there's nothing to lose.
In every breath, a new wonder creeps,
In the silence of the enchanted sleeper's keeps.

Rides with Wandering Souls

Through the mists of the silent night,
We ride with souls, hearts taking flight.
On winds of whispers, secrets spread,
Each journey begins where others tread.

Together we drift, in moonlit grace,
Chasing echoes in this sacred space.
With every turn, a story unfolds,
Of ancient tales and dreams retold.

The starlit road beckons, wild and free,
With every heartbeat, we feel the spree.
Connected through realms, our spirits blend,
In the twilight glow, we shall transcend.

As dawn approaches, the journey slows,
But the bond we share forever grows.
In the tapestry of life's shared goals,
We ride along with wandering souls.

Milton Keynes UK
Ingram Content Group UK Ltd.
UKHW021929011224
451790UK00005B/83